Calamities and Cuddles

Written by Beverley Smyth

Illustrated by Cheryl Coville

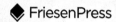

Suite 300 - 990 Fort St
Victoria, BC, V8V 3K2
Canada

www.friesenpress.com

**Copyright © 2021 by Beverley Smyth
First Edition — 2021**

Author and Dedication photos courtesy of Kayla Photography, Kayla Hannaford. Illustrator photo courtesy of Karen Coville of Karefree Photography.

All rights reserved.

No part of this publication may be reproduced in any form, or by any means, electronic or mechanical, including photocopying, recording, or any information browsing, storage, or retrieval system, without permission in writing from FriesenPress.

ISBN
978-1-5255-9938-5 (Hardcover)
978-1-5255-9937-8 (Paperback)
978-1-5255-9939-2 (eBook)

1. JUVENILE NONFICTION, BIOGRAPHY & AUTOBIOGRAPHY, HISTORICAL

Distributed to the trade by The Ingram Book Company

Dedication

This storybook is dedicated to my grandchildren, who are growing faster than grandma can write her stories.

Thank you, Isabelle and Mitchell, for being my inspiration and for filling my life with love, giggles, and joy.

Love Grandma

Calamities and Cuddles—Grandma's Story

My story is about a little girl, an only child, who grew up in the 1940s on her parents' dairy farm, located in rural eastern Ontario. Though part of a loving family, this little girl used her creativity and imagination to make a world of wonderment for herself.

I was that little girl. This story begins when I was five years old, and at that time, my biggest wish in the whole wide world was to attend school in the one-room, country schoolhouse. But I had to wait another year, until I was six years old, for my wish to come true.

Our little farm was tucked away at the end of a very long and bumpy gravel laneway, so there were no houses and no "next door" children for miles around . . . so it seemed. How would I cope with the loneliness of having no other children to play with for another whole year?

In the summer, the farm was surrounded by fields of green grass, and in the winter, it was surrounded by snow—lots and lots of cold, wet snow! The farm was my playground, and being an only child, the farm animals were my playmates. My four-footed friends included the spirited workhorses, Prince and old Queenie, my faithful border collie, Ring, a little pig named Oink, and a woolly lamb called Lamby.

I still chuckle thinking back to my silly antics in those days when I decided to cut my blonde ringlets, or the Sunday afternoon when Ring and I danced in a road puddle while I was wearing my Sunday best clothes! I know my mother was often both angry and disappointed with my behaviour. Perhaps the word "exasperated" best described my mother's feelings, and she said that she never knew "what possessed me" to behave the way I did.

Calamities and Cuddles is a collection of nostalgic stories—precious vignettes—from my own rich memories and oft-repeated stories from my loving mother and father. Their nurturing love and stability enriched my upbringing, and the experiences they provided helped to shape my whole life and made me realize that I was indeed a lucky little girl.

My Wish

More than anything else in the whole wide world, I wished to go to school. In those days, children in my community went to school in the one-room, country schoolhouse located in Glen Buell. It was near busy Highway 29, the main highway between Brockville and Smiths Falls.

My parents often reminded me of how anxious I was to begin school and to have real friends as playmates.

One morning, I came downstairs wearing my newly washed blue denim overalls, my favourite red and blue checkered blouse, and a blue ribbon stuck in my messy blonde ringlets. I pulled on my tall rubber boots, for playing in road puddles, and picked up one of Father's big milk pails. I announced to Mother and Father that I was ready to go to school today!

Mother quietly explained that I was still too young to start school and would have to wait until I turned six.

Another whole year!

At five years old, I could already read the comic strips, which we called "the funnies," in the weekly newspaper thanks to Grandpa's time and patience. I could print almost all my letters with my right hand. And I could ride a big horse. Surely I was ready for school?

Ring

My very special, four-footed playmate was a handsome border collie called Ring. Ring was named for the swishy white ruff of fur around his neck and chest. He was a working dog on our farm and recognized for his adeptness in herding cows and rounding up sheep. The farm animals paid close attention when the collie was about, or a nip on their heels would remind them that he was boss.

Ring was a gentle collie and my constant companion when not needed for farm duties. I adored Ring.

Father had fastened a rope swing from the big maple tree in our front yard. Whenever I swung higher and higher and Ring was about, he would dash back and forth under the swing seat, barking excitedly!

Ring and I whiled away many hours playing in the front yard of our farmhouse. While I played, in my loudest voice, I often sang out the rhymes that Grandpa Kendrick and Mother taught me: "Miss Polly had a dolly who was sick, sick, sick, and she called for the doctor to come quick, quick, quick!" There was also "Little Bo-Peep," "Baa, Baa, Black Sheep," and several more that I remember.

Mother loved hearing loud singing in the front yard. It was a good sign to know my whereabouts.

If I could not be found in the house, in the front yard, or around the farmyard, Mother would have her suspicions that Ring and I were up to no good. She only hoped it wouldn't lead to some calamity!

Prince and Old Queenie

I don't ever remember being afraid of the farm horses. Of all the heavy, four-footed farm animals on our farm, my father's team of work horses was my favourite.

I was never afraid when Father hoisted me up on Prince or Queenie's back and I heard their soft nickering sounds of welcome. I always remembered to have several apples squeezed into the pockets of my blue denim overalls. The friendly horses loved McIntosh apples and would gently pull them off my outstretched hands with their velvety-soft lips.

Father often told the story about the time he was watching me while ploughing in a small field near our house. I was astride old Queenie when she suddenly stopped before passing under a low tree branch that could have brushed me off her back.

Mother told me later that she could not watch me ride the horses for fear that I would slide off their backs and be stepped on or, even worse, trampled!

Later on, when I was older and Queenie became too old for farm work, Father retired the old mare to a grassy meadow, replacing her with a graceful dapple-grey horse named Buddy. When Prince and Buddy were not working in the fields, Buddy became my "pony" to ride along the country roads and to fetch the cows for milking time.

The Barnyard

From a very early age, my parents talked to me about how to behave when around the farm animals, especially the cows and horses. "Just don't surprise them!" they said. The barnyard was no place to be for a little girl and her dog. I had been warned often enough *not to go to the barnyard by myself*.

But I did . . . just this once!

I was not quite strong enough to lift the heavy bar on the barnyard gate but managed to climb over the rail fence that surrounded the barnyard. Ring squeezed between the rails, and we both landed in the barnyard with Father's black-faced sheep and the ram.

That day, the old ram was being particularly watchful over his flock, and when I started to cross the barnyard . . .

BAM!

The ram charged and knocked me to the ground! He continued to knock me down each time I struggled to my feet. Ring's frantic barks brought both Mother and Father running from the barn to rescue me from what could have been a very sad accident.

My parents told me how frightened they were and that I could have been seriously injured.

Father and I sat in his Morris chair by the big picture window for a long time, quietly talking and cuddling.

Coboss, Coboss

My father was very proud of his beautiful herd of black and white Holstein cows. They produced an abundance of fresh milk, which was sold to the local dairy plant in Brockville.

Father and Ring would fetch the cows from the grassy pastures on our farm property. I would hear Father's booming voice call out, "Coboss, Coboss." He was telling the cows that it was milking time and encouraging them to be standing ready at the pasture gate. If any weren't listening or moving fast enough, Ring would nip at their heels. It was the collie's job to help bring the cows all the way to the barn for morning and evening milking times.

Sometimes, I would come along with Father and Ring, but it was a long walk to the back pasture for a little girl. The walk was often an adventure that required careful footwork to avoid, what Father called, "cow-ploppies." Cows don't worry about where they leave their droppings. However, the long walk turned into a fun ride back to the barn when Father put me on Belle's back and walked alongside the gentle cow. Father thought it best if we didn't mention this to Mother, who would have worried about me tumbling off the back of the calm and gentle cow.

Mother was the best at milking cows. She sat on an old three-legged stool, leaned her head against the cow's smelly belly, and hummed under her breath. Mother said the cows would wave their ears towards her and "let down" their milk.

My parents were strict about my coming to the barnyard by myself because the farm animals could be very unpredictable. However, during milking times, I was allowed to be in the barn with my parents. I played with the cuddly barn kittens and liked the way the cows watched me with their glassy large black eyes.

I discovered that, like the horses, the cows also liked McIntosh apples. The cows would wrap their long rough tongues around my hand and the apple at the same time, which made a rather slobbering mess. I could never cram enough apples into the few pockets of my overalls to please all the cows at once. This sometimes led to a dispute among the cows and would upset Father's milking routine.

Always in a Dither

I was never certain how the geese arrived on our dairy farm or why. They were bothersome and seemed always to be in a dither, wanting to be somewhere, anywhere, most of the time.

The geese could not be trusted, especially the sassy old gander. It was Ring's job to keep the geese away from the farmhouse, away from the colourful flowerbeds, and especially out of Mother's much-prized vegetable garden.

Of course, it seemed the geese snatched every opportunity they could to zigzag across one of Mother's favourite flowerbeds, usually leaving a path of trampled flowers behind. Mother would be terribly upset with the silly geese and vowed to take revenge on the geese by locking them in the barn.

I knew exactly what my mother meant by the word "revenge," for I too had good reason for wanting my own revenge. On one occasion, the old gander loudly hissed and flew at me for no reason. He chased after me, flapping his huge wings, and nipped me on my bum. OUCH! After that, I always kept Ring close to me whenever the geese were about.

I could hardly wait to see what calamity the geese would cause before they were locked up in the barn. What would Father say?

Devious Woolly Critters

The sheep were a worry. Father was always thankful to find them contentedly nibbling grass in the front pasture close to the farmhouse, but our flock of black-faced sheep could certainly be stubborn critters with minds of their own.

Father said the sheep were profitable to our farm's income, with their healthy yearly "crop" of spring lambs marketed every fall. The sheep were also sheared of their wool coats in the spring, and their wool fleeces were packed in huge bags to be shipped by train to the woollen mill. There, the wool would be processed and woven into fine woollen blankets to snuggle under on bitterly cold winter nights.

The springtime antics of the lambs were so laughable. The bigger lambs would clamber up on the large rocks in the pasture and challenged each other, bunting each other off the rocks! The smaller lambs bounced about in play without a care in the world. The fat, saucy lambs were the first to be sent off to market.

The sheep were truly headstrong. When one sheep found a small hole in the old rail fence to push its head through, soon the entire flock would follow. They would poke their heads through to the adjacent field, rich in clover and alfalfa, and nibble grass where they shouldn't. Eating clover and alfalfa could upset a sheep's tummy, causing it to become sick, sometimes so sick that, in a few cases, the sheep would die. A disastrous calamity!

It was Ring's job to quickly round up the sheep and lambs and bring them to the sheep shed. Father must have been quite tired of repairing the "poked out" holes in the old rail fence.

An Old Shoe Box

My father always kept a flock of black-faced sheep in the front pasture nearest our farmhouse. There would be great excitement every spring with the arrival of each baby lamb, sometimes twins. During the spring lambing season, my parents would make numerous trips, often in the middle of the night, to the sheep shed to help deliver the new lambs.

If a newborn lamb became separated from its mother ewe for a certain length of time, the ewe would abandon her lamb, leaving it helpless and hungry. Father would be there to scoop up the lamb, wrap the little fellow in a warm towel, and carry the lamb back to the summer kitchen.

Mother would be waiting with a warm bottle of milk and an old shoebox warming on the oven door of the old wood-fired cook stove. The hapless little lamb would be placed in the shoebox and immediately given a large spoonful of Father's special medicine. Together, the medicine and warm milk performed miracles. In no time, the feeble little fellow would be struggling very hard to stand up in the shoebox.

Father kept his miracle medicine on a high shelf in the summer kitchen, out of reach of little hands. I somehow recall the large lettering on the big bottle spelling out "S-e-a-g-r-a-m-'s."

The stray lamb was kept in a tall, straw-filled box in a corner of the summer kitchen and bottle fed, usually by Mother. Sometimes, though, I helped. Some springs, there would be several orphaned lambs in the summer kitchen. When the lambs were strong enough, they were returned to the sheep shed to "steal" milk from the other mother ewes.

There would always be one pet "Lamby" trailing me around the farmyard and Mother's front lawn. One time, a lamb walked through Mother's new summer kitchen screen door—Mother was not pleased!

The Little Runt

One early spring morning, our closest neighbour appeared in our farmyard. Farmer Shea was holding an old grain sack in his hand and talking to Father.

In my imagination, I can still see the old grain sack shifting about, up and down.

Ring was wild with excitement, dancing round and round, sniffing at the old sack. I thought I could hear soft grunting sounds coming from it.

With a warm handshake, a deal was made between the two long-time neighbours. The next thing I remember, a very small pig tumbled out of the sack! This was not a fat, porky pig, but a scrawny, runt-of-the-litter piglet that would require many bottle feedings and perhaps a spoonful of Father's miracle medicine. Farmer Shea knew that we would provide a safe home.

Mother suggested we keep the piglet in the summer kitchen for a few days before sending him out to the barn to join the farm animals. I helped Father prepare a box filled with straw, while Mother warmed a bottle of milk. The piglet snuggled into my arms and very quickly sucked and slobbered down TWO bottles of warm milk. With little grunts of contentment, the pig nestled into his bed of cosy straw. Much to my joy, there was a wee piggy living in our summer kitchen, and very soon, this little pig became my pet Oink.

This Little Pig

I waited until my parents were preoccupied in the front parlour, listening to their favourite radio show, *The Jack Benny Hour,* before I would quickly bundle up little Oink and slip quietly up the stairs to my bedroom.

The little pig enjoyed rooting and snorting about in my soft woollen blankets. He loved to have his little fat belly scratched while I read stories from my picture books—possibly stories about the adventures of three little pigs and a very scary, hungry wolf.

After a while, my parents would realize the house was much too quiet and that I was missing. Mother's quick footsteps on the stairs meant the jig was up for Oink. The little pig quickly rejoined pet Lamby back in the summer kitchen.

My mother's patience soon wore thin after finding the little pig rooting around in my bed several more times. That was when Mother "laid down the law," threatening to send Oink to the barn—immediately!

Oink's days in the summer kitchen were numbered. I worried that the little pig would be stepped on by Father's fat cows or trampled on by Prince or Queenie, which would have been a dreadful calamity.

Frilly Bonnets and Pink Bloomers

I think my mother preferred her little girl to remain in the house, entertaining herself by dressing up her Christmas dolls for afternoon tea parties or wheeling the dolls about the front yard in a stylish green wicker doll carriage, which once belonged to my dear cousin Lois. But that was not always to be . . .

I remember those early summer days with my two wonderful pets, Oink and Lamby, that gave me so much joy but my mother, a few headaches.

Mother insisted my pets be healthy and scrubbed clean of barn smells. This meant Oink and Lamby would be lye-soaped in warm water, heated in the copper boiler. The pets strongly objected to bath time and were the cause of several small floods in the summer kitchen. Thankfully, Mother just laughed.

One day, Mother was standing out on the front steps, admiring her beautiful flower garden, when I wheeled the green wicker doll carriage around to the front yard. Oink and Lamby were riding in the carriage, dressed in doll clothes. The pets were wearing frilly bonnets and bright pink bloomers pulled over their hind legs.

Suddenly, the geese appeared, zigzagging across the front lawn towards Mother's beautiful flower garden. Ring began barking his head off in hot pursuit of the bothersome geese.

Meanwhile, Oink and Lamby jumped out of the carriage and toppled onto the lawn. Both made a fast getaway while still wearing their bonnets, their pink bloomers gone with the wind.

What a hilarious *calamity*!

Scrambled Eggs

Mother was in charge of the large white-washed henhouse full of soft clucking hens. Father was wise to leave the management of the hens to Mother's wisdom and capabilities. Mother was thrifty with the money earned from selling fresh eggs and dressed poultry at the Saturday morning Brockville Market.

Mother quietly explained the reason I was not to go in the henhouse by myself. I would upset the hens and "put them off" laying their eggs. However, I certainly could help from time to time with feeding and gathering the eggs. Ring was not allowed near the henhouse.

The day I unlatched the henhouse door, I was carrying a big milk pail and Ring was trailing along beside me. Perhaps I had in mind that I was helping Mother with the chore of gathering the eggs. Or perhaps I let my curiosity get the better of me.

When I opened the henhouse door, Ring squeezed past and bounded in, disturbing the soft clucking hens. As this was a new experience to the collie, he immediately began herding the very surprised hens into a corner of the henhouse, and his incessant barking terrified them!

Through the ruckus of squawking and flying feathers and straw, I struggled to pull the eggs from their nests and "gently" drop them into the big pail.

SPLAT-SPLATTER! SPLAT-SPLATTER!

It didn't take long before Mother appeared at the henhouse door. It did take some time, however, to calm the hens. Mother was sure her soft clucking hens were so spooked they would never lay another egg! A calamity for sure.

After that, I received a scolding from Mother and a reminder when scrambled eggs with bits of eggshells were served for breakfast.

Father quietly replaced the old henhouse latch with a new, much stronger latch bought at Landon's General Store. Father said the new latch would prevent robbers from stealing any of Mother's eggs and gave a wink in my direction.

Changes

Lamby soon lost interest in following me around the yard and chose to join the other lambs playing and bouncing about in the front pasture.

One Saturday morning, I waved goodbye to the lambs as they were loaded into the back of a truck destined for the market. The fat and saucy lambs and, yes, Lamby were playfully bouncing about in the back of the truck as it drove out our bumpy long gravel laneway to Concession Road 6 and, finally, busy Highway 29.

As usual Ring ran alongside the truck, barking with great excitement. The collie would always turn-tail when he reached the end of our long laneway.

Meanwhile, Oink very quickly outgrew his straw bed in the summer kitchen. Father built a special pen for the growing pig, near the barn, where I could visit him every day. Oink still enjoyed having his back rubbed and being scratched behind his ears. Mother made sure that Oink had plenty of apple and potato peelings for breakfast, dinner and supper, along with his daily ration of mash.

And so, Oink began to look more like a porky pig every day.

The Empty Pen

One day, Ring and I set off to visit Oink, only to find his pen empty. That was a very sad day.

I asked Father about Oink's whereabouts, but really, I knew the answer before asking the sensitive question. Father knew that I would be heartbroken about the loss of my pet Oink. He too was sad about the fate of the pig that had grown from a wee runt to a fancy, fat porker.

With much sadness, I remembered the happy times Oink and I had together, when I hid the wiggly little pig under my quilts and scratched his little fat belly while I bottle fed him warm milk, and the numerous visits to his pen with a small pail of peelings, always gobbled up in one big slurp.

It was true that Oink had almost outgrown his special pen.

My thoughts lightened when I remembered dressing Oink and Lamby in pretty doll clothes and wheeling them about the front lawn in the green wicker doll carriage.

For a long time, I refused Mother's wonderfully prepared pork roasts and savory pork chops and would have a good long pout during mealtime.

Indeed, a sad but predictable farm calamity.

A Dangerous Habit

There were times when I moped about our farmyard, with Ring trailing along beside me. My farm friends did not always make me feel happy, and I put on my best pouty face for Father, who would tease me. As I was a fancy farm girl with messy blonde ringlets and a blue bow stuck in her hair, he called me "Little Miss Pouty-puss." Perhaps, being the centre of attention to my parents, I was spoiled.

Father's teasing went too far one day when he handed me one of Mother's salt shakers with instructions of how best to catch a bird. Ring and I spent an entire morning trying to catch birds by tossing salt on their tail feathers. My frustration ended in tears. Thankfully, Mother came to my rescue and explained that Father was just playing a little joke on me.

My father may have been a tease and a "push over," but he had a soft place in his heart for his little girl, who wanted so much to have real playmates and to begin school. On occasion, when I would put on a long pouty face, Father and I would jump in our old blue '37 Plymouth and drive to Landon's General Store. There, Father would spoil me with an enormous strawberry ice cream cone.

Whenever we drove out of the farm, Ring would race alongside our car, barking his silly head off with excitement, until we reached the end of our long gravel laneway. Our beautiful, gentle collie would then return for home. But chasing cars was such a dangerous habit!

No matter how hard my father tried to "break" Ring of the habit, it was of no use. Father would just shake his head and sadly mutter that he was afraid the dog would "meet his Waterloo" one of these days . . . whatever that meant.

Father did not offer much of an explanation, but it didn't sound like a happy meeting. More like a pending calamity!

Ice Cream

Landon's General Store was prominently located on the corner of two dusty country roads in the small village of New Dublin, about a twenty-minute drive from our farm.

On a Saturday evening, the general store would become a gathering place for the villagers, the local farmers, and the folks in the surrounding countryside for shopping, the country gossip, and treats.

To the eyes of a little girl, Landon's General Store stocked a huge assortment of EVERYTHING. The tall shelves behind Mr. Landon's enormous counter were crammed with grocery supplies. The counter was covered with assorted chocolate bars and colourful candy of all flavours—some three for a penny. Houseware items, boxes of sticky flycatcher strips, and men's work-boot boxes overflowed the store aisles. People took up positions on the wooden nail kegs on the far side of the store to chat with one another.

Yes, Landon's General Store had everything, including ICE CREAM!

Mr. Landon lived up to his reputation of serving the biggest ice cream cones in the whole wide world—for a nickel!

I would quietly perch on a nail keg, licking my gigantic strawberry cone while Father and Mr. Landon discussed the local gossip.

Concession Road 6

One day, Ring and I started walking down our long gravel laneway. I had been wearing my new tan sandals, but walking in them was slow and uncomfortable. Small sharp pieces of gravel kept getting stuck in my sandals and between my toes.

My parents warned that it was unsafe to walk out to the end of our laneway. It certainly seemed safe enough when Father and I went for a strawberry ice cream cone.

I hadn't gone far before Mother caught up with me. I suppose she had been watching out the big picture window of our home when she spotted me walking slowly down the laneway with Ring.

Mother was very angry and said that I deserved a spanking! Since I did not remember ever being spanked by my parents, I was unsure of what to expect.

Mother broke off a few stocks of goldenrod growing by the side of the road and began hitting the backs of my legs all the way back to the house. I cried! Mother said that she cried too. Then we cuddled.

Time passed, and I asked Mother why she did not let me walk down our laneway. Mother said that army vehicles were allowed to use part of Concession Road 6 to practise maneuvers, and because it was a dirt road, the tanks would create great clouds of dust. A small child would never have been seen. This was a wartime calamity.

Army tanks never appeared on our part of Concession Road 6, and in my memory, the army vehicles were never mentioned again.

A Farmer's Wife

Mother loved all things beautiful and orderly—our farmhouse, the colourful flower gardens and plants surrounding the farmhouse, and her well-tended large vegetable garden on the plot of land next to the henhouse, home to her happy hens.

Mother was a wonderful cook and baker, winning praises for her fruit pies and cookies. Her apple pies were the best, and lemon pies, a close second.

How did a farmer's wife ever prepare for a dozen threshers or corn cutters with less than two days' notice? Mother would have pies baked, a milk pail full of potatoes peeled and mashed, and several roasts of meat ready for hungry men with huge appetites. They would enjoy two hearty meals, both dinner and supper, before moving on to the next farm the following day.

Farmers rotated from farm to farm in a cooperative effort to harvest the grain fields and cut the corn stalks into silage to feed the cows over the long winter months.

Every year, Mother would carefully make and label jars and jars of preserves and prepare bushels of potatoes and McIntosh apples to be kept in our cool, dirt floor basement for safe keeping over the winter.

Time with Grandpa Kendrick

Grandpa Kendrick visited our farm every year. Those two months were joyful times. I always knew when Grandpa was about to arrive by train from Toronto. There would be a great flurry of preparation while getting freshly washed sheets, goose feather pillows, and soft woollen blankets ready for the spare bedroom. It was so important to make Grandpa's stay as comfortable as possible.

Being a wonderful cook and baker, Mother always had a special rhubarb cream pie and soft gingerbread cookies waiting for Grandpa's arrival.

My special time was spent perched on Grandpa's knee for endless hours, listening to him read "the funnies" in the *Family Herald and Weekly Star* newspaper. My kind, patient grandfather would read the comic strip cartoons over and over again to his favourite "little one" sitting quietly on his knee. I would say, "Just once more, Grandpa."

My grandpa, with the twinkling blue eyes, read many stories to me—sometimes expanding the stories and nursery rhymes much to my delight and enjoyment. My mother's worries were few during Grandpa's visits to our farm. She never had to look far to find me.

Unfortunately, Grandpa Kendrick never visited our farm after I started school. I clearly recall my father standing me on a chair in our summer kitchen, putting his arms around me, and gently breaking the sad news that Grandpa was very ill. He soon passed away.

My parents tried very hard to fill the space left by Grandpa with plenty of cuddles, but it was never quite the same. I will forever be my grandpa's "little one."

These are the special grandparent memories that you just can't forget.

The Big Chill

Every fall, when the leaves were gone and a big chill filled the air, my family moved from the summer kitchen into the main rooms of our farmhouse. The move signalled the coming of winter and a somewhat slower pace of farm life.

At this time, Mother would cook on her new Findlay Deluxe stove that she helped purchase with money earned from selling fresh eggs, dressed poultry, and a variety of fresh garden vegetables at the Brockville Market.

I think Mother chose the Findlay stove for its fancy oven-door handles, a gauge to register oven temperatures, and a built-in side tank for heating water. It was known as "the reservoir." The Findlay stove also provided additional warmth to the downstairs rooms.

We relied primarily on the coal-burning furnace in the basement to heat our two-storey farmhouse. The radiation of warmth from a single pipe that snaked its way from the downstairs to our upstairs bedrooms helped keep us warm through bitterly cold winters. The annual taking-down and cleaning of the stovepipes was a terrible, messy necessity. Unfortunately, the pipes could catch on fire if the black soot was allowed to collect inside the pipes.

My mother's heavy-knitted socks felt so cosy and warm on our cold floors. Father would be up stoking the coal in the furnace during the coldest of nights, as our farmhouse was no match for the chill that descended upon our bedrooms.

I often danced my fingers through the layers of frost that formed overnight on my bedroom window.

Mother would tuck a hot water bottle under my sheets after we said our nighttime prayers together. I would quietly whisper my own prayer, just loud enough for Mother to hear, that I wanted a pony for Christmas—a pretty pony with a long flowing mane and tail. Perhaps this Christmas?

Christmas Dinner

I never quite knew what to expect in my Christmas stocking. A lovely big orange? Sweet, striped candy canes? Or perhaps a hunk of coal? That was one of Father's little jokes.

Christmas morning, Father would carry me downstairs, bundled up in my cosy woollen blanket, and prop me beside our lighted tree. This year, I worried that Santa Claus might think I was an ungrateful little girl, wishing for a pony and not the usual pretty dolls left under our Christmas tree.

There were presents under the tree, beautifully wrapped in red and green tissue paper with tiny gold ribbons. Mother excitedly directed my attention to Santa's present . . . another doll! This was a life-sized doll, very beautiful with soft golden curls peeking out from under her frilly bonnet. She had long eyelashes and sparkling blue eyes that opened and closed when I rocked her gently back and forth. This was certainly a special doll, as it cried, "Mama!" I named her Wendy.

There was no pony, though. Perhaps next year? Even though we had Queenie and Prince, my biggest disappointment living on the farm was not ever having a pony to ride around the farm and help Father and Ring fetch the cows for milking time.

My eyes lit up when I read Santa's note thanking me for leaving a glass of milk, a soft gingerbread cookie, and several carrots for the reindeer.

Mr. and Mrs. Lawson, Bunny and Clara, were my parents' dearest friends and were always invited to share Christmas dinner with us. The Lawsons had no children.

Somehow, this dinner seemed more special to Mother, who had cooked, baked, and roasted for several days on her new Findlay stove in preparation for Christmas Day dinner. It certainly was a splendid Christmas feast. The Lawsons heaped praise on Mother's roast goose, stuffing, mashed potatoes with gravy, vegetables, cranberries, mincemeat tarts, and berry pie. I was delighted and got all giggly inside thinking about the roast goose. I was more than happy that Mother had finally put an end to one bothersome goose—hopefully, it was the old gander. What a wonderful calamity!

Winter on the Farm

During the winter, the farm animals enjoyed the comforts of a warm stable and were fed and watered twice daily. There was always a good supply of hay and grain for Prince and old Queenie and for the sheep wintering in their shed.

The cows munched on hay, grain, and the corn silage brought down from the tall silo. The cows still required milking twice daily but gave little milk this time of the year.

Mother's hens were lovingly cared for over the winter, enjoying plenty of grain, fresh straw, and the whispering of many soft words.

Farm life was not always easy for my parents, as they had daily chores to perform. Farmers cannot take vacations. However, the winter months brought an overall slowness to farm work, allowing more time for leisure and more time for me. After farm discussions, planning the coming spring, my parents now had plenty of time to read the *Family Herald and Weekly Star* from front to back.

Mother wrote letters and could be found in the front parlour, reading a favourite book. My mother taught school before marrying my father and had to adjust to the demands of farm life.

Mother always looked forward to the arrival of the seed catalogues and deciding on interesting new vegetable and flower seeds to add to her gardens.

We had a tall radio, perhaps called a console. My parents especially enjoyed listening to comedy. *The Jack Benny Hour* and *Fibber McGee and Molly* programs were their favourites. BBC news broadcasts and musical programs were also part of our daily lives.

I remember quite clearly the galloping hooves of the Lone Ranger's horse, Silver. I was not allowed to listen to *The Shadow* or *Boston Blackie*, but I did anyway!

Collecting the Mail

One of my best memories was going to get the mail on snowy days when sky-high snowbanks filled our long laneway.

Father would make the usual comment about the snow being much too deep to make it out to Highway 29 with our old '37 Plymouth.

Quickly, Prince was harnessed and hitched to our farm cutter, and away Father and I would "fly" along the laneway, down Concession Road 6, to arrive at our mailbox on Highway 29.

Once in the sled, Father would pull the smelly old buffalo robe right up to our chins to keep us warm and cosy for the snowy trip. I would close my eyes and listen to the rhythmic jingle of the cutter bells and to Father's soft clucking sounds of encouragement to the heavy-footed workhorse plodding tirelessly through the deep snow drifts.

Our mailbox was the largest and shiniest of all the boxes at the corner of Concession Road 6 and Highway 29. One spring, starlings insisted on building a nest in it.

We would find the *Family Herald and Weekly Star* waiting for us, and perhaps a letter for Mother or Eaton's Catalogue.

The Spitfire

In winter, the fields crusted over with drifting snow and fences all but disappeared. This created a magical, snowy playground for a little girl, her dog, and her red Spitfire sled.

Ring had a lot more time to spend with me during the winter, as he was not needed for farm duties, like herding the cows or rounding up the sheep. The cows were contentedly munching hay in the cow barn for the winter, and the sheep were comfortable in their large sheep shed.

Father fashioned a special harness to hitch the collie to my Spitfire, and away the two of us would "fly" over the crusty fields of snow near our farmhouse.

There would be the odd nasty spill but never a real calamity.

Mother worried if a real calamity should happen, she would not be able to come to my rescue. The deep, crusted snow could not support Mother's weight, and she would sink up to her knees in deep, wet snow.

During these winter months, I could be assured of high drifts of snow forming against the side of our house—perfect for tunnelling. I would often spend an afternoon digging tunnels with my little red snow shovel while talking to Ring.

My mother would make numerous trips outside to be assured the tunnels were safe and not about to collapse. Mother also brought treats—my favourite sugar cookies and hot chocolate.

A Right-Handed World

My mother was skilled in all facets of needlework, from knitting pretty sweaters and crocheting doilies to fancy needlepoint and embroidery work. Some winters, she would host a quilting bee in our front parlour for the neighbourhood ladies.

Mother's attempts to pass on her sewing skills stalled when she discovered my left-handedness was an impediment to her instructions. Mother believed in a right-handed world and insisted on tying my left arm behind my back at mealtimes. I had mastered printing the letters of the alphabet with my right hand by the time school started.

To this day, my handedness is a concern, as I have a history of closing kitchen drawers on my right hand.

I managed to "knit two, purl two" for a very nice winter scarf for Ring. I was cautioned to keep the scarf short, or the collie's front paws would get caught up in the wool and Ring's red scarf would be torn to tatters.

Mother's sewing basket spilled over with a plethora of buttons in all shapes, sizes and colours. Sitting next to my mother as she sewed, I would often sort these buttons using my left hand when I thought Mother wasn't watching.

These were cuddling up times spent with Mother.

The Shirt Off His Back

My father was so kind-hearted and generous that he was known to give "the shirt off his back" to his neighbours.

Father often loaned out his farm machinery to the younger farmers in the local Glen Buell farming community. Unfortunately, sometimes, the machinery would be returned bent or broken. The hay rake would have a broken wheel, or the mowing machine would be worn out from overuse.

Mother would be quite upset and scold my father for his generous habits, but he continued the practice of lending out his farming equipment as a means of survival for the younger farmers in the community.

I don't remember my father lending out his new Cockshutt tractor, which was partly paid for by the sale of two of his best Holstein cows. However, Father would give a neighbour a day's work with his tractor, sharing the demanding workload of farm life.

The Little Scallywag

Mother "laid down the law" about bringing barn cats into the house. But, when she added that Father was not fond of cats, my curiosity got the better of me.

One Sunday afternoon, I spotted our barn tabby with her wee kittens in the farmyard. Everyone knows kittens are soft, cuddly, and loveable. I carefully picked up one of the wee kittens and ran to the house. Mother was preoccupied in the summer kitchen, and Father was enjoying his customary Sunday afternoon nap in his favourite Morris chair by the big picture window. Quietly tiptoeing up behind Father's chair, I yelled, "SURPRISE!" and dropped the kitten on his shoulder!

Well, my father flew off his Morris chair, like you wouldn't believe, while batting away at a very frightened bundle of tumbling fur. Mother came to rescue the wee kitten. Father gathered his breath, sat down in his Morris chair, and continued his nap. No one said a word.

Mother and I quickly returned the little kitten to its mother, and very quietly, my mother offered an explanation about Father's behaviour. "Perhaps, your father had a frightening experience with furry animals when he was a young child."

Mother laughed and called me a little "scallywag" for playing such a naughty trick on Father. Mother and I always had a good laugh telling the story about Father's funny experience with the kitten. Father pretended to never hear our teasing.

Fewer Calamities

Finally, September arrived, and I was old enough to begin Grade 1 in the one-room schoolhouse located in Glen Buell.

Mother helped me select pretty clothes from Eaton's catalogue. I was excited when a large package, wrapped in brown paper, arrived in our big silver mailbox. Mother often told me that I looked very pretty that morning, wearing a nice white blouse, plaid skirt, red sweater, socks, and brown shoes. My blonde ringlets were freshly curled.

Mother sent me off to school with a kiss and a big hug. Father called me "Little Miss Fancy-puss" and pretended to hide my new lunchbox in a big milk pail.

Mother and Father said they would miss their little girl.

After recalling my mischievous behaviour back then, I wonder if perhaps a feeling of relief came over my parents when they said good-bye to me on the first day of school. I'm sure there were fewer calamities.

Mother promised to keep Ring secured in the summer kitchen when Father and I drove off to school in our old blue '37 Plymouth.

I discovered many children that first day of school. Children my age to play with at recess time. The girls and boys in Grade 1 would be my friends forever. I remember my first-grade teacher, Mrs. Sequire, with much fondness. She was impressed with how well I could read and print my name using my right hand.

A Final Calamity

Later that September, I knew that something bad had happened when Father appeared at the school door. He and Mrs. Sequire spoke in hushed tones at the back of the classroom. Father found Ring lying on the side of busy Highway 29. Somehow, he had escaped from the summer kitchen, and my faithful collie had followed our car to the busy highway.

Father guessed that Ring had finally "met his Waterloo" by way of a fast-moving car. We buried the faithful farm dog under a McIntosh tree in our orchard beside the house. Father fashioned a small wooden cross to mark Ring's grave.

My parents understood my great sorrow for the gentle collie and allowed me to remain home for lots and lots of cuddling.

Later, I told my parents that I imagined all the farm animals came to the orchard to say their goodbyes to their special four-footed friend.

I was sad, but I was also so happy to have shared a profound friendship with Ring. I had finally started school and was making new friends. However, I would never forget my mother, father, or farm animal friends and their unconditional, everlasting love.

In memory of my husband, Gale, who brought his laughter, his wisdom, his thoughtfulness and his gift of love to his family and grandchildren.

With Love

Acknowledgements

Expressions of gratitude to:

Jean Francis, for helping to format the manuscript and integrate the illustrations. Jean's suggestions and support have been very energizing for the completion of this project.

Mara Brown, Director, Carleton Dominion-Chalmers Centre, for inspiring me to raise the "bar of excellence."

Dear friends, Dorothy Pratt and Laurie Slaughter, for being supportive critics. All the personalities mentioned in *Calamities and Cuddles*, who impressed my young years in meaningful ways.

My sons, Greg and Brad, for their interest, encouragement, and support in this project.

CPSIA information can be obtained
at www.ICGtesting.com
Printed in the USA
LVHW061610060721
691977LV00004B/393